TABLE OF CONTENTS

I. *CHIAROSCURO*

II. ILLUMINATION

Crayola Can't Make These Colors

...from the palette of a life in verse

To Genoa City Library with my personal gratitude for keeping minds and books alive

Elaine Madsen

CRAYOLA CAN'T MAKE THESE COLORS...
...from the palette of a life in verse

Elaine Madsen

13 Hands Publications

Los Angeles, California

Original cover art by Elaine Madsen.

"Crayola Can't Make These Colors... from the palette of a life in verse"

Designed and Edited by Michael P. Naughton & Donna Novak
ISBN - 13: 978-0-9767260-6-7
ISBN - 10: 0976726068

LIBRARY OF CONGRESS CATALOGUE IN PUBLICATION DATA
LCCN: 2008910878
 9 8 7 6 5 4 3 2 FIRST PRINTING

13 Hands Publications
914 Westwood Blvd. # 518
Los Angeles, CA 90024
www.13HandsOnline.com

Also visit: www.ElaineMadsen.com for more information.

INTRODUCTION

Crayola Can't Make These Colors is a collection of poems, which allows the reader to take a journey with the poet. An excursion through early tragedy, with its accompanying grief, anger, survival and final renewal, is written in a dignified but honest way. Elaine Madsen explores solitude, depression, betrayal, joy, friendship and motherhood with passion. She leads us, finally, to the wider world, exploring such events as 9/11 and war.

The book contains instructions on healing without moralizing, strength without preaching. Ms. Madsen confronts her own mortality in a way that transcends. Fearless, her shifting voices create a canvas that would be otherwise unattainable.
One of the most powerful pieces is the title poem, which celebrates special people in her life, with a language that is rich and full of seductive sound.

> *She's dragon dreamed wishes and*
> *tigerskin platinum, set in a gem*
> *of satinwine themes. She's a dancer of*
> *fire-iced peaches that burst open flooded*
> *with music she grew for the*
> *crucible life spilled in her way.*

These six lines exemplify a poem full of exciting, tight language, jam-packed with appreciation. Amazingly, she sustains the poem throughout 4½ pages.

Another memorable poem is "Bookplate Secrets Revealed at the Newberry Library." This piece encompasses mythology, biblical references, literature's greats, history, science and nature with originality and depth.

The organization of the book is done in a painterly way. There is, in many of the poems, an undeniable elegance of rhythm. The poet's wisdom is exhibited throughout the book. Life-lessons are brushed on from the palette of a woman's life. As though in an art gallery, we wander distances with her to the light.

—Ellen Reich
author of *The Gynecic Papers and Reverse Kiss*

*With gratitude for that unknown place
from which poetry comes unbidden
demanding to be heard.*

CHIAROSCURO

"The instruments of darkness tell us truths..."

— William Shakespeare from Macbeth

JANET FRAME'S NIGHT AT THE OPERA

Images cascade from the specks
of black on white paper,
from her store of memories?
Must be. How else
        to have traveled
        from her paper/pen/ computer
        to the mail to the desk
        of whoever accepts fiction
        at the New Yorker
        and recognized the
        luminous truth of it.

Such lush specks of black,
deliberately inked on the
pages in my hand have left
their mark on the specks of
my memories of days behind
doors which opened only
        from the outside.

The Hospital Called

"Come right away,"
           We arrived.
           We verified our name.
The nurse said: "I'm sorry, the baby's gone."
I said, "Gone, where?"
           I was eighteen.
           I didn't know babies died.

Grief, there and then, made a nest for itself,
in the aerie of my soul where joy was meant
to flower, but instead forever limns its edges.

While joy does come, 'tis never unalloyed;
and always is imposed upon by the saw-toothed
edge of grief, obliterating boundaries that
never smile; feeding forever on the meal
it continues to make of my soul.

We Were an Accident/The Three of Us

Gus and the baby and me
happened accidentally
and the fallout of the grief this birthed
sucked us into a wake that swept us
away; for the bloom our baby was meant to be
was birthed with a heart that took his life.

Nor could the nights of the days that
scourged themselves upon the mistake
that we had made, make something true
out of our marriage, or ever deliver one
moment of comfort upon our grief,
              of which we never spoke.

DEATH MUST BE A LONELY SOUL

Death must be a lonely soul,
it's rarely asked to come.
It might improve its image
                some;
if it would change the way
                it does.

Death did not come
    in a smoky mist.
    Instead it came
        like T H I S —

            tearing out my backbone,
            wrenching out my eyes
            in a silent demolition.

Death does not hurt the one
    it takes, for that I have been
    grateful. But those Death
    does not take are left
    behind— like so much
    fruit smashed on a wall.

Irrevocable

Grief is a knife that scars life's face
and makes time taste
      of melancholy;
      erasing itself
      of tangible trace,
except for the marks it
leaves, indelibly,
          on soul
          and faith.

For Death stays on, our tenant,
never leaving us alone,
never leaving us a thing
to help us understand,
especially on days when
one's cup runneth over.

TASK AT HAND

I was annoyed by the task at hand, which was,
that day, to write a note of condolence to a student
whose mother had died of something socially
acceptable. I was at that time plotting my own demise
which would have been socially unacceptable.
My words to the girl would not commit themselves
to tidy lines, but leapt away in random bits of crushed-up
paper strewn about my feet like flowers of evil, blooming
too brightly in the gloom of my office until I heard them
shouting about the lie in the lines I was writing.

The lines I wrote, were not a note to her, but were instead,
a mirror in which I saw my three children bereft,
not bereft of the loss of the failure I felt myself to be;
but bereft by the loss of the only mother they had.
And I was shamed. And then I screamed at Life
which would not accept my resignation. "All right,"
I screamed, "I'll stay! I'll stay! But only until
they do not need a mother anymore."

And then I wrote, a proper note, to my student
who would never know it was her loss that made
me see my task at hand that day had not been
to console, but simply to stay, and simply to last;
so my children would grow and never know,
I'd almost left them alone. The days of all the years
I've lived since then have become, more times than
I can count, when my "task at hand" is simply to be
joyously present at moments I'd have missed,
but for the note Life would not let me write.

DEPRESSION

It is as if my eyes are blind
and I've been cast upon a wild sea
with no knowledge
of what boat or sea can be;
and I dare not break free, 'tis…
only drowning waits for me.

Scream, Heard

Rape is the ultimate impotence, all but terror dies.
The reward of survival concealed from me how
my silence sucked rage like a Black Hole in space;
a rage that could not be expelled, and could not
be expressed. The scream I did not use that night
would have been for his amusement, there on
the ground in that ravine, where only trees and snow
would have heard. I remained mute all the years
that followed, cowering in frightmares of stolen
sleep that refilled the well where the terror lived.
I dared not speak of it. Who would want to hear
                                        a scream?

And, after all, I was not murdered; he did not leave
me there, in that ravine, to be covered by snow
and never found. Wasn't it enough, that I had lived?
Wasn't it petty to also ask to have my voice back?
So, I didn't ask. Rage went on eating my soul,
sucking in grief for the voice I had been; while
I smiled, and soldiered on, as if it was nothing,
at all that had happened. For, after all, I was
nothing, and only nothing, on that night, in the
snow, on the ground, in that ravine. So, rape
continued, on its own, in the black hole, where
                                        my voice had been.

Until today. For here, on this page, my scream
screams. And screams out loud. For on this page,
                                on this day,
                                in this room,
                                my voice
                                is heard, at last.

Sisyphus Sister

I've looked at Death, I boasted aloud; and Death,
once seen, is simply —There.
I have borne the worst of pain –
I've strength enough for anything.
Truth was – Death wasn't – only There.
It shadowed and muted my will.
Whenever my womb was growing life,
Achilles weakness was growing, too.

As the fruit of my womb began to mature,
that shadow paled, but remained all the same.
Until I read a philosopher's words –
She said "We all live in fear, fearing Death."
"Not I," I said, "I'm not afraid to die.
I chose to live, when I wanted to die."
The shadow on my will spoke out --
"The word isn't die. It is Death."

I protested, "There's no difference."
"But there is," spoke the shadow again.
"You do not fear the dying of *you*,
You fear what Death does while you live."
The shadow was right – I did live in fear,
I'd fought a battle with Death every day
since Death smashed my first-born's life.

Each day, Death arrived, quite like the stone,
which Sisyphus pushes forever in Hell.
Each day my children lived, I rolled it away.
Each morning they waked, it was There.

I covered that stone with many a guise,
a costumer, consummate, I. But, now
it lay naked, grey and exposed;
exposed by the glare of those words.
Its surface was worn by the press of my hands.
I touched the places where they had been;
and found beside the sign of my palms,
the marks of three small pairs of hands.

A Forest Fire is a Waste

For thirteen summers, we built
bridges made of matches, near
a forest fire, over rich monotony.
When they had been consumed,
I looked across at you, and knew,
with dreadful clarity, the fabric
of the matches was my soul.
On my remaining limbs, I
                    crawled away.

Sunset in Black

I watched the sounds the colors
made while their ribbons warped
the rain into a desert,
on a canvas
made of
dried-up
willows
dying
in the
eyeless
images
that will
never see
because,
my Socrates,
you died
before
I'd lived
long enough
to know
I was
so wrong.

Beyond Control

There was a time when I was God
and measured out my days
choosing just how much I'd keep
And what I'd cast away.

Drunken on the wine of choice
I resigned my sceptership.
Time assumed its majesty
and I went out to live.

Time's reign was unremarkable.
So silently did it rule, I no longer
paid it heed, until today;
When time, inevitably, levied its tax.

The silent monarch demanded
its due be paid in a random
event no one can ever predict
and no one ever prevent.

DISSONANCE

All alone, I've built a wall
of excuses, apathy.
The mortar is self-pity,
        it towers over me.

Outside this wall are rainbows,
I have heard their echo.
Outside this wall is music,
        I have seen its shadow.

The winds of life blow freely.
I only see them pass.
The scent of growing spirit
        has slipped between my hands.

From the hollow of my soul
in anguish I cry out,
"Help me know reality,
        O God, I want to Be."

Night Train Travel

The Night Train's ticket is written in depression,

pronouncing its provenance with invisible ink

drawn from bleeding illusion and the glare

of presumptions, leering in the neon fog

surrounding the station at which you alight

in a foreign land, unnamed until you enter

it and find there are no maps, not even a schedule

for when the next train back to daylight will appear.

But you will, nevertheless, recognize

this property upon which you disembark.

It is sown with events over which you had

no control and where your own deliberate

actions and inactions have flowered now

into the tracks upon which your

night train prowls its endless course,

until you abandon the province of

regret for full frontal authenticity.

THE TEACHER

Words cloak my experience
and the verses I fashion of them
are done with the hope that their
shaft of light will last long enough
for you to see beneath them,
but, now I see, what you ask
                    of me,
                    is to be —
                    the light.

SALVATION

By tiny bits and pieces
I'd given me away,
    to time and things
    and people 'til there
    was nothing left one day.

I reached out my clenched hand
and opened it to see, the one called
friend place in it, a tiny bit of me.

You Can't Unsay What's Been Said

Rage and fear and unresolved
pain, balanced themselves like a
cobra poised on a stone, with
fangs razor-thin, slashing the
face of my trust in us into
shreds which may not heal.

Your apology was worse than
the wound of your words, for
it opened up old wounds, deeper.
"You fucked up, big time." you said.
      O, did I ever.
But not the way you think you know.
I fucked up thinking I could do it alone.
I fucked up believing anything is possible.
I fucked up not knowing it's too late
to start a lifetime of work
with less than half a lifetime left.

But, you don't know about that.
You believed I could do anything.
What stirred your rage was your
first sight of finding out I couldn't.

WHEN JONATHAN WAS FIFTEEN

In the big white house with the broad green lawn,
Everything was certain, everything was right.
No one needed to ask. Everything was there,
But, no one ever talked.
No one stopped to listen.
Most certainly,
No one heard the whispers Jonathan made—

"Do be certain, Jonathan to—   *I wish...*
Bring me home good grades   *— can't ...*
Do be home on time,   *— you...*
Do not forget your keys,   *— please...*
Turn out the lights, and don't forget   *won't you...*
Church is at eleven...
You do look nice today, dear,
But wouldn't blue be better?   *help me....*
Have you finished your report?   *— please....*
Don't forget your meeting.   *— I'm....*
Your activities seem to be
Suffering, Jonathan.   *...tired—*

Darling, are you listening?

Jonathan?

Jonathan?"

On Thursday, Jonathan hung himself

To keep his screams from getting out.

Shrapnel

Suicides may think their act a private one,

designed to end a private hell.

But, suicide is not.

Instead it starts another hell,

or five or ten, for

        suicide's irretrievable,

        its acid sears the bone

        of everyone who's left behind.

Mass murder is what's done.

ILLUMINATION

"They told me night and day were all I could see..."

— *William Blake*
from the Visions of the Daughters of Albion

BREATHING INSTRUCTIONS

There are wounds which suppurate
and sap your strength, unless
you remove the shrapnel lodging
      in the lungs of your soul.

Removal is a language
which you must inhale
before the infection
      owns the rest of you.

This language is the oxygen
of recognizing
that you are more
      than the wound.

Refusing to inhale will make you,
like the witch from Oz,
"…really, most sincerely dead."
      Breathe deeply.

WEATHER WATCH

Beware of men and women who are neat;
the tidy souls who cheerfully
and seriously
arrange the shelves of life
until there is no room for it.

And, simply ever after,
rearrange its little pieces
in and out of little bins,
and neatly package sins
into air-sealed little tins.

While you stand outside
in the icy rain
all shivery and wet;
looking in at all the warmth and light
hoping they'll have a rummage sale
and maybe they'll find some room
for your own little bins
and your own little tins.

So, you've got to remember to run like hell
whenever it rains and keep on running
'til it stops.

Archeologically Speaking

Selective vision makes the past

so much prettier to drown in

than the necessary moving on;

sans map,

sans road,

sans visible destination.

It would be so much easier to sink

here, to ignore the light ahead;

it may be, after all, only a mirage.

But if, instead, it's destiny out there

and not just the comfort of the past

that I would have, then I must go;

sans map,

sans road,

sans visible destination.

Discovery

Passion, untamed, like a wild horse,
is capable of nothing but the endless
pursuit of the wind; 'til it dies
exhausted, an impotent carcass.

Passion, tamed, however, can run
on many plains, can be renewed
and does not die in the witless
splendor of the wind.

Like a wild horse, I ran, with conviction
born of terror, believing that to bridle
even the passion of my mind meant
my very self could then be broken;
but, one of my passions has been tamed,
and I am not broken. In fact,
to my surprise —
> I am still whole; and strangely,
> find that I am being fed.
> I did not know the wind
> I sought was starving me.

Deconstruction Blueprint

The boundaries imposed by convention

have porous and seedy edges, where

we are tested when we push against

them, on attempting deconstruction.

Whether you tap-dance, slash-and-burn,

burrow beneath or leap out in faith, you

will only remain unscathed, if you stay

where you are and tear pieces from

your soul to feed Convention's rules.

DECEPTION

At first, deception's a sliver of ice

that does not melt; because it has

the strength of a gene,

doubling itself and redoubling again

until it's the heaviest thing you own.

The Palette of My House

I write in my brick-red office,

read in my goldenrod living room,

cook in my kitchen of burnished peach,

    and sleep in my lilac-hued bedroom.

The palette of my house lightens the charcoal shadows

    Fate scrawled across the walls of my life.

MYSTERY

Mystery attends our every breath,

from the first one to the last.

For some 'tis but an enemy,

requiring anesthesia;

others follow its siren song

and encounter revelation.

THE GUISES OF FEAR

Fear once controlled me;
until I saw its two faces.
One demands escape;
The other pauses
        to recognize.
Both point to flight.
One stifles life, the other
leads to it. Take heed
of its origin — before you run.

BETRAYAL

Betrayal first stabs out the eyes
of trust and history,
then, slowly drips its acid in the
empty sockets, to verify the wound.

Haiku

Barren, impervious and
stark, the trees hide their
secret from winter.

MEMORY

Unasked for, memory spurts through a crack
in the pavement of the day, or bolts through
a knot of unresolve,
like the jagged smell
of close-by lightening;
and, sometimes,
it
just seeps,
like first-light,
beneath the
barred door of resistance,
to seize us brutally.
Or,
sweetly;
while feeding itself
on our acceptance of its intrusion.
Then,
it returns to the mystery of its existence,
restoring itself, while lying in wait for its
next decision.

On Charles Bukowski

At your own risk,

dare to walk

another time,

on the streets

in Charles Bukowski's mind.

Their intersections with your own,

take out their knives

while you're away

and insist

on cutting new ones,

                deeper.

OVER A MARTELL AT THE CARLYLE

The days and nights numbered with our names

are stark and rich,

disappointing, too much, and never enough;

for we count them knowing those numbered

with the names we love have been marked

by Time for itself.

Realité

Realité revealed in evanescence
                is bearable,
but the brilliance of its apogee
                is too terrible
                                to see.

A Word with Baggage Got in the Way

There was something that I wanted you to know,
        something that you taught me,
but as I formed the thought of telling you,
you used a word, unknowingly,
that comes with baggage you did not
assemble and that word stopped
me from telling you, you'd given me a gift.
Tamed was the word you used.
For me its synonym was "broken."
Climbing over your word has taken
two days, but now I'm on
its other side, and I have made,
a discovery.
I want you to know
that what you taught me
matters.

When Going On Beyond All Reason

When going on

beyond all reason,

you will need your boots;

and you must hold your hand,

yes, your own hand...

the one with the

Buddha's eye.

A WOMAN IN HER PRIME

A woman in her prime, can't be
rearranged to suit your design,
her boundaries haven't geometry.

She understands the distinction between
what she wants and her needs
and relishes the economy.

She is, for the patron of theatre,
the delicate difference between
effervescent and evanescent.

Her strength was forged on an anvil
cast of failure, grief and triumph
tempered with humour's leaven.

There is a kind of madness at her core,
where the roots of her passions grow,
and no mathematician can ever go.

The melody she used to be,
is now a full-scored symphony,
self-composed and self-conducted.

The music she's become,
can't be played or danced or sung,
unless you've a composition of your own.

ON BEING SEVENTY-FOUR

Inside every old person there's a young one
wondering, "What the hell happened?" I don't.
Because I know. Exactly what happened.
I lived, I wept, I failed, and reinvented myself
more times than I knew I could; lived in a
mansion and in two little rooms and in
everything in between.

When I was very young, I couldn't find people
who had anything to say, so I manufactured some
           — three of them.
Because of my three children, I've had more life to live
on some singular days, than some live in a lifetime.

I've known great love and loss
and grief, much more intimately
than I'd ever have wished,
but in its darkness I discovered
the riveting end to the argument
I once had with God.

I've been composing the symphony
of my life for seventy-four years.
I'm now on the theatre movement
with no last movement in sight.

ADVENT

The first Advent came unannounced
heralding unexpected joy.

Sometimes so arrive
the advents
of our lives.
Be Watchful!

PARADIGM

Light illuminates
a night,
a heart,
a mind.

It sometimes comes
in a love,
in a hate,
in a Star.

But it is only seen,
when it can find
an open place
where it can shine.

Ashberry'd She

She is the author of 'grin and bear it.'
She is the master of all she purveys.
She is sobriety, tipsy with whimsy,
she is a giant, malaproped quote.

She is a twilight tattoo of Tabasco.
She is an irony whistling a prayer.
She is a triad reciting credenzas,
she is the nightmare's Gemini'd joy.

She is an expert on cycles and seaweed.
She is astride the wristwatch you treed.
She is a fanciful cream puff of questions,
she is the one who puts ice in your beer.

She sings for voluptuarian cattails.
She dances aboard the dandelion's kite.
She dampens the desert with oysters d`jour,
she cancels an earthquake with crystal-eyed dyes.

She strangled a gnat one night in Rangoon.
She pitched a senator secrets in tune.
She balled the King of the Afternoon Moon,
she baked him today in the green tea lagoon.

She stepped over petulant pipers in pastry.
She twirled from the top of a biped kazoo.
She ravaged an icicle painting a monkey,
she's gotten equipped with double-deck boots.

She sees the whole Louvre in a cardinal's feather.
She canned all the gerbils asleep in the hall.
She once seduced a barbecued winter,
she axed a whole river of radiant fleas.

She's wrathful and wonder-eyed, sleeps in canoes.
She watches for oxcarts in pink ribbon heels.
She let out the spiders dressed in green sugar,
she laced up the string beans spliced without heir.

She yawns with aplomb and never is tired.
She tap dances deftly with Tarot-timed mice.
She climbs under anthills to entertain turtles,
she teaches Antartican envelopes dice.

She is denouement, laughing in cartwheels.
She will take orders for needlepoint dust.
She is behind you, leading your footsteps,
she is an innocent, insolent bitch.

PERSPECTIVE

"In a fabulous necklace, I had to admire the anonymous string by which the whole thing was strung together."

— Dom Helder Camara
from The Desert is Fertile

SOCRATES

I remember when I had no body
and was only a formless dream.
I lived in a hollow silent shell
consumed by flame
and numb with shame.
Your hearing and teaching
tamed the flame and clothed
 it in direction.

With word and touch and time
you built a temple
where no shame can live.

My eyes and mouth and breast
you drew from the sunlight
of your giving.

The temple's newly darkening gate
became for both
of us an invitation;
written with old, forbidden words
as the blooms we strew
in the field of passion.

Until passion mounts in a boiling surge
cleaving the furrow where your sons
are sown in the garden you fashioned
from a silent shell.

GLANCES

You and I do not need to harden
feelings into words. Instead
    your eyes
    hold mine
    and send
    ribbons
    of sun
    draping over my breasts
    curving down my body
    coiling into a spreading
    ball of warming wanting.

I HAVE MEMORIZED YOUR HANDS

I have memorized the lean and squareness of your
hands, stretching into fingers full of searching sun,
commanding springing, surging warmth with words
which have no shape, pressing sound all through the
empty echoes of my breasts, to waken up my nipples
from their trance, until they sing into your palms
that you must trace your hands across the hollows
and lift my empty mouth into the feasting of your own.

GENESIS

Behind the curtain, formed a play,

while the authors played at forming one.

The curtain rose before it was done,

      "A faulty conception," the critics announced.

The authors reflected, undecided

on their newly discovered surprise

Just as curtains descend without any

warning, in the very same way, they rise!

LEFTOVER WINE

Undressed, we paused and poured
two glasses of wine, so we could
talk a little first, but our eyes caught
in our pulse, our mouths forgot the
wine; as you slowly dripped a stream
of it between my breasts, watching
my eyes watch your mouth smiling
at the warmth it spread in me while
your hands found my warmest place
and opened it to drink the wine
my body makes from your touch.
Waiting your return, the stoppered
bottle watched me from the shelf
for three full weeks; I hesitated
to open it, for left-over wine can
go sour, sometimes, just as memory can.
Finally, curious, I poured a glass;
                its color was still clear,
                its fragrance was still true,
                its flavor was still rich,
                like this memory of you.

IT COULDN'T HAVE STAYED THIS WAY

It couldn't have stayed this way, of course,
because of who we are. It might have become
one of those once-in-a-lifetimes you never
erase and pay the price of, forever.
If I were younger, I might have damned
the ruin to have the splendor, accepted
the cost; but, if I were younger I wouldn't
know what I know now, about such a cost.
And I don't have the strength to pay it.

SUNRISE IN ATLANTA

Morning arc'd out of a greystone slash,
devoid of definition;
only a moment of night's remission.

Rapt, in your arms, "No sunrise," I mused.

> "Not true," said you;
> "I'll show you where chiaroscuro
> and color well from a palette made
> of images shared; and, delicate,
> balancing, merging thought with
> long-dead dreams,
> can be given form
> on the far-away side of reason's space,
> where intimacy can limn our lives,"

was what you whispered into me.

TRILOGY

I.
A sound held its breath
and touched the air;
then shattered into pieces,
of which you made a melody,
to play inside my silence.

II.
The fabric of our passion
is spun of incandescence;
we celebrate its claret hymn
inside its saffron bloom,
suspended in a cameo
of passion's intermission.

III.
Enclosed in the sanctuary
of resplendent detumescence,
I feel as if you are my pulse,
come coursing through my veins;
my limbs are simply half of yours
in consummate communion.

A ONE-ACT PLAY

A powerful one-act was what we had,

the action took place in our beds.

But last night it moved to the

stage of my mind where I breathe

and sing and I didn't know it would

feel like that to have you there.

From the wings I saw how the next

act would go and I wept, for it can't

be; this has to stay a one-act play,

life's ordered it closed, out of town.

MONOLOGUE FOR TWO

"I know and love a part of you, the part of you that's poet
I fear the part I cannot see, veiled with something dark.
Is it a scrim that you designed to foster an illusion?
Or curtain drawn to center, awaiting an overture's cue?
          Can the scrim be taken out?"

          "Will there be a curtain call?"
                    "Will there be a review?"
          "We'll know by the Early Edition."
                    "Can't we decide for ourselves?"

"We could query the composer, the producers and the writers;
we could question the director and interrogate the crew."

"But it's we who are composer, director and the crew!
 It's we who are producers, and the writers,
we're an audience of two!"

          "Who the hell writes the review?"

          "Maybe it's still rehearsing?"

          "Has it closed?"

          "Is it being held over?"

          "Where is that Early Edition?"

          "I don't think Variety covers these things."

SLEEPLESS NIGHT

You buried your mouth in mine
and opened a well of feeling
that had been holding its breath
so long I thought it had expired;
but there it was; erupting
in a geyser of surprise,
that kept re-issuing itself
and denying me sleep
for more hours than
I want to admit.

THE MUSIC MAN

My body was a monotone
that spoke just to itself
the notes I had forgotten
were turning into stone.
I'd hidden in my mind
the key in which to sing;
the Music Man knew where
it was. The rhythms of his
body grew new notes where
there were none. I learned
to play duets and we wrote
the orchestration for a symphony
that only we could play.

GIFT OF THE SEA

You gave me an ocean as blue
as deep silence and at once
as light as a lark singing new.

You gave me an ocean as green
as new rain and at once
the shade of an aquamarine.

You gave me the ocean's
windforce, stinging our faces,
racing the storm to the harbor.

You gave me the ocean's memory
sealed in a seashell's mystery.

You gave me new eyes so I
could see the sealife ballet
'neath the ocean's surface.

You gave me a sunset writing
her verse in pink/golden clouds
for the night sky to hear.

For my delight you reposed
on a table, the bright orange
opera the flame tree composed.

You gave me your laughter,
your time and your joy and
told me the truth of your loss.

You gave me the now that is all
we're allowed and I have become
something more than I was.

OTHERNESS

There was a quality in you, for which
I had no name but by which I was intrigued.
This quality explored with curiosity
                sans questions.
The curiosity seemed compliment;
       asking no approval,
expecting to be accepted, but
subtle enough to recognize
       when it was not.
I interpreted this as quiet assurance
       rather than arrogance.

I asked if you liked to dance. You
replied "Can't you see that I am?"
I didn't see 'til later, you were telling
me that, you only dance with yourself.
I didn't see that you were playing Pool,
'til I was in the side pocket, wondering
                where you went.

SALVAGE

The pantheon where I enshrine
the men I loved and left or lost,
was invaded by a tidal wave
as I prepared your installation.
The torrent of your betrayal
flooded through just in time
before I'd placed the raw clay
of happiness into the kiln.
I'm ankle deep in detritus, but
the sun is pouring in. You didn't
belong there. How did I miss that?

My pantheon is empty now.
The pedestals whereon I'd posed
those who were particular have
fallen from neglect. Yet, even in
this dust, lineaments of some remain
in verses I wrote which do not deserve
                                        erasure.

UNEXPECTED AFTERNOON

There must have been an afternoon
I felt I was complete.
There must have been an afternoon
I could recall as sweet.
If there has been, I've lost it in the
wonder of an unexpected afternoon.
Discovering that I have been
charmed.

INTERIORS

"I feel in my heart a strange place, a part of me that's lost..."

— Michael Madsen
from The Complete Poetic Works of Michael Madsen

Dandelion Dusted

I climbed to the top of a dandelion,

      and found you hiding there.

We lolled all over the golden fluff

and came down

to find people stare!

I don't know why they act that way,

but, on the other hand, I've never seen

any other fuzzy, yellow ones like

      me and thee.

The Aquarium in Chicago for Your Birthday

We saw at the exact same moment how
the sea turtle mines its own oval seams
in the dreams of the Sea Teller's Song.

But, at the Aquarium, the sea turtle
circles, gone slightly mad, but slyly
amused at being served and now,
                    being safe, from Man.

CRAYOLA CAN'T MAKE THESE COLORS

Cheri's an exquisite lemon-light, golden bright dream.
She's dragon dreamed wishes and
tigerskin platinum, set in a gem
of satinwine themes. She's a dancer of
fire-iced peaches that burst open flooded
with music she grew for the
crucible life spilled in her way.

Michael is magic-hour's purplenight blue;
he's a silver–edged featherflight, sungreen festooned.
He's a luminous lark,
with a scarlet streaked brow,
that's sown with a star from the Pleides' bow,
where it's growing new stars
for their Michael to throw.

Virginia is volatile violet, golden champagne,
an amethyst fragrance with witch-willowed will.
She's a crystal of velvet-hued lavender eyes,
dancing upon a dandelion song,
the mistress of magic's indelible sign;
An indigo innocent,
incandescently timed.

Bish is mellowed maroon with golden grained green;
he's hummingbird haloes and tigerlined moons.
He's darkened seclusion, he's blue bloomed and true
to family-formed heart signs
which play steel song strings;
on harp-ripened roses
and gilded balloons.

Nicky is boldfire red and vibrant
magenta; he's streaked with cerise
and full of a promise that glows in
the dark and shoots into space,
creating the dream he was born
to fulfill, growing new love
to live in our hearts.

Alex is lavender, purple and white,
awhirl with a sparkle, aloft on balloons.
She's the color of loyalty, written in Runes,
she's dancing to music she's
painted in rainbows
she grows in her garden
of wintergreen dreams.

Gina is pink, she's white and she's
full of sweet dreams and giggles
that squeak, and roll down my cheek;
she's an appleripe red that briefly was
darkened 'til she redirected and
now is ablaze with the coral and
gold of joyful intention.

Christian is steel and cobalt blue;
he's a mystery writing a song in
silvery language only he knows.
He's history's nephew, he's newly etched awe,
he's a mirror of honor that sits over there
on the branch of a tomorrow
he's grown for himself.

Max is a willow wand
jousting with time,
afloat on anthems
of pearl-borne questions
he found in a jungle
which questions
the concept of sense.

Jack is the color of domino rainbows,
silvered with snowsongs, abloom
with an emerald of starshine and crimson,
imagining how it would be, to be blue.
He's curious, he's merry, he's an arrow of
joy; he's innocence written
in wisdom's new dreams.

DeAnna is woven of rose wondered time and of
satin tomorrows, building blue timecastles moonkissed by
fragrance that lilies and aloes have promised
to grow when they've cleared out the
cobwebs of fissured grey winters they've
strewn in the way of the green blossomed
springtime she plants every day.

Hudson's a river that swells
with new tides raging with
wonder, rising each day
on the back of a question
he hasn't yet found,
running on splendor,
aloft on a dream.

Kalvin's the color of sunsets,
a gold and blue promise;
he's made of the nightsong,
a laser that's arching its way
to the moon, wrestling with mystery,
plowing new seeds
in the garden of truth.

Luke is fresh water,
crystalline blue,
an open door to a
dreaming dawn
where planets of poetry poise on
the wings of his future in colors
that no one has seen.

Marisa's an opal,
glowing within.
Streaked through with mystery's
song; she's discovered a joy as
Nick's Queen of Hearts,
bearing a bloom of the
life they have flowered.

Evan's aglow in the heart of
old seas, composing new tide
and the windsong's new dream.
He's a ballet of laughter,
and dancing new rhythmns
to weave in the gates
of geometry's grace.

Nate's made of starshine and morning's first grace;
he's an island of strength
cloaked in midnight blue mist
made of infinite care
and unconditional love which he
gives to all in his circle of light.

Maya's a promise, pink as the dawn
in the fresh blooming joy, a moment
of wonderment dancing the rhythm
Time has composed
for who she will be.

MOTHERING

"Fly on the wings of the wind, my darlings,
fly in the arms of dreams. Fly to the ends
of the earth, my darlings, on the wings
that I've fashioned for you."
They were wings made of picture book snows
and pumpkins we carved and stories we read,
with lullabies echoing Valentine songs,
and Christmas and birthday surprises.
With your license to fly you made trips
to the vaults of heartbreaking deserts, skipped
upon mountains that spit open flame, while
you learned how to fashion wings of your own.
When I found feathers molting from
the wings I'd designed, I muttered
and worried and stuck them back on.
You, in your love, permitted that sometimes,
while painfully lifting them off yet again.
And when you were gone, you left those behind.
"How will you fly, what have you done?"
"Mom, can't you see we've grown wings of our own?"
Once I cleaned out the cobwebs I'd built
from feather dust, glued shut with time;
I could see that you have, yes indeed!
They're marvelous, marvelous, look at you soar!
exploring the back of the moon and the inside of night,
tasting the sun drops, in charge of your lives.

Though I cheered your flights on, my own wings
grew weary. I cut them off; and flightless,
I mourned for who I had been, begging alms
from myself in yesterday's tears. My wings
had a mind of their own, and in spite of myself,
kept regenerating and trying to fly.

Imagine! New wings! Where shall I go?
I don't have a map or a reason to fly.
But there was no map when I dared
to embark on the flight which birthed
my children; and clearly, these new wings
are not ornamental. So I took a test drive
of an orbit or two and found out all over,
whatever is out there, this time on my own.

In learning to use these new wings, I did
not always prepare carefully; nor did I see
that those flights weren't properly charted.
Sometimes I fell. And there were my
grown up children, patching my wings,
waving me on, cheering me home, before
we set off for whatever comes next.

FOR TODD ON RECEIVING HIS DOCTORATE

Butterflies cannot divine the palette
in their wings; and therefore cannot
celebrate the visual feast they are.
An act of celebration requires one's
self-consciousness; that we bestir
the silent eye behind our daily lives.
I do not know and cannot celebrate
these accolades, this adulation,
this approbation of your peers.
I celebrate instead, the crackle of
your mind; your pithy wit and ruddy
laughter, commitment to ideals. I
celebrate your questions which would
not accept my easy answers, demanding
that I reach for ones to challenge you.
I celebrate the Grace that let the separate
loops of time in which we dwell to overlap
so that we've become, one to the other,
                                        friend.

As Lois was In October

I remember reading once of a clinic,
where people go to learn to die.
Do they think you just get used to it
as one does to waking up?
I choked away the thought, that this
is where I've come. I let the thought
come out again, to reveal the way
the thought of that eats into my mind.
The pains in my body can be subdued
by the stock in their chemist's chest.
They use their tools to peer
at the stuff of me they can count,
on scans and charts and graphs;
while I am wont to wonder about
the stuff of me that has no weight,
not a single degree or a beat.
Is there DNA for Curiosity; a genome
of Ideas; or an RNA of Love?
There's more of me in them than there is,
in what they chart; for these are what
have never been killed, by tyranny,
weapons or law. So, if those things
can't end and I am in them,
can it be that neither do I?
But, where do we go, these things and me?
To some sort of unnamed sea, where it all
gets renewed, to emerge once again,
to counter this world that keeps
counting itself — on charts? I wonder.

As Lois Became in November

I found a cartoon in the New Yorker today
that I knew would make you laugh and I
reached for scissors to clip it out, but
before they were in my grasp, I realized
you can't laugh. Not this time.
Not any time. Not ever.

The message is still on my voice mail.
"Lois died, I'm sorry." No details, no
nothing, just "Lois died."
But, you're not dead, you're not!
You're sitting right there, there in your chair.
and you and I are entranced yet again
by Michael Jordon's aerobatics.

We're eating ice cream and decrying
the failures of the politicians who ought
to know better and especially those who don't.
We're talking of the verses we'll write
when words stop hiding from our pens
and we're reading to each other the ones
we did write with the words we were able to find.

We're remembering again, on other days,
the men who made us warm and the ones
who made us cold, worrying again, and rejoicing
in, the lives of the children who've graced our lives
and grew up before our eyes. We laughed at irony's
witlessness; and puzzled the ponderous which has
no answer to why the world even IS, after all.

In this town we knew would have buried
our minds; we've kept each other's alive
and wrenched open the door to each
other's souls where we'd hidden the grief
that never ends and O, my friend, my
dearest friend, how I hate that now
there are things I need you to hear
but now can't say – not ever.

But I salvaged this one little moment,
when I saw the cartoon and believed
you were there and would laugh at it
with me. And for that one moment,
                              you were.

We, neither of us, have patience
with religiosity, so there be no prayer
to ease your loss, but I hear you yet,
                    reminding me:

> *"You've still got time, Girl,*
>   *You've still got time,*
>   *use it well!" was what you said.*

Okay, Girl I'm trying
          but, it's so much harder,
                    alone.

JAY

It said in the paper
he was born and died,
had brothers and sisters,
a wife and two girls.
                    They told about his job.

They forgot to say
he had grace and wit
and humor and heart
that he cared — so much.
                    No room for that.

They forgot to say how he cared
for those the people in power
would have liked to forget;
and they didn't remember to say,
                    sometimes, he won.

They couldn't have known
he knew life was absurd;
that he pointed it out
so wryly and well, especially
                    when he'd lose.

They couldn't have known
he knew life was rich,
that he relished its tastes,
and savored its shades,
                    with passion and joy.

Life ebbed slowly from his grasp
because he held it so very fast
and stole some of it back,
each time it slipped away,
        to give to all of us.

They didn't tell how much he touched;
how much he gave and how he grew,
how much we gained, how much we've lost,
but, it doesn't matter that they didn't tell.
                        We knew.

Too Much Too Soon

"You're the man of the family now,"
I said, thinking to make him proud,
not knowing this was confusing
when he was already confused
about his parent's divorce.
I didn't know a boy of eleven
mustn't be asked to be a man,
especially when he already
knew he could never be
the one his father expected.
I gave him a box of tools he
didn't know how to use either.
In time he learned how to be
his own man and to master
any tool you can name.
I got to bandage some of the
wounds, but nothing erased
                    the scars.

HORIZON LINE

"It is the courage of our questions which gives us the truth of our answers."

— *Steve Mason, poet laureate of Vietnam veterans from "The Human Being"*

National Security

The acid of our betrayers drips drop by drop
from media's mouth via airways which
once belonged to us; but were given away
for entertainment; while they busied themselves
writing plays titled *National Security*.

Though we who protest are vigilant, our eyes
are no longer safe. Our Bill of Rights has been
infected with a virus concocted by the Department
of Justice. She is no longer blind with honor,
she's been drugged by the *Patriot Act*.

The betrayers of this nation bear the banner
of liberation, parading it before what
they think are our sightless eyes;
unaware we see clearly, the Robes of Power
we placed on their shoulders have been
exchanged for the garments of Fascism
force-feeding us the pornography
of war disguised as *National Nourishment*.

September 12th, 2001

Behind the yellow tape,
jaws of giant cranes
lift away the carnal rubble,
pawing at debris,
seeking fragments of the lives
borne aloft
in chalky smoke,
bearing our horror to heaven,
spreading to the everywhere
that's left the smithereens of lives
now stopped in an
                    incalculable forever.

Beyond the yellow tape
wait loved ones
left behind,
for whom there exists
no crane to lift the grief
come to dwell in their own
                    incalculable forever.

Anyway

The skyline

 of New York

that remained

after the eleventh

of September,

towers

so nakedly

against the sky;

yet fills

each day with people

who dare to work

there anyway.

ELIOT'S PHOENIX

A Phoenix rose from Eliot's Wasteland
composed of light so brilliant, it
printed shadows on a wall in Hiroshima.
Scavenging in Giverney for the fragments
of the world he'd lost, Eliot labeled what
was left "The Wasteland"; unaware that it
was compost for the Phoenix Flowers of Evil.

From the fragments Eliot found, the Phoenix
reassembled on a desert made of melted eyes
oozing out of blackened sockets, as it walked
on miles of corpses, carpeting camps where
gates declared to those arriving that "Work
will make you free"; while smoke from human
flesh coiled out of chimneys venting ashes which
fell on Nine-Hundred Days of Moscow graves.

The ashes from those ovens have been chronicled
so carefully, in belief that such a vista could never
come again. But, the Killing Fields of Vietnam,
Cambodia and Rwanda, Somalia and Bosnia are
living coals, lining the uterus where the Phoenix
Fetus waits the signal for contractions to begin.

In Congo and Darfur, on the streets of New Orleans,
from Baghdad, Teheran, Gaza and Televiv,
on the mean streets of L.A., intolerance for differences
spews forth to make committees, with breath enough
to push those living coals to tongues of flame,
which will feed that unborne Phoenix. Pray
God it be stillborn. It can never be aborted.

LONDON

I saw from the top of St.Paul's
Tomorrow pronouncing itself
        in a graceless cell phone tower.

I saw, in a St.Paul's crypt
Lord Nelson's remains, uncomforted
        by Lady Hamilton's remembrance.

I saw, in Shepherd's Market, joy clattering
by on my grandsons' skateboards
        making their own history heard.

I saw in the British Museum, national
hubris blinded -- Assyria's winged
        monuments tethered for amusement.

I saw in the halls of the Tate,
an artist's thought holding its breath;
        Turner's paint box awaits his return.

I saw, from a boat on the Thames -- Time,
re-posing my question: "Where am I,
        on my personal space-time continuum?"

LOS ANGELES HAS TAR PITS

The Tar Pits which L.A. hides, have melted in the heat
of burning passion, spent by worn-out souls who did
not see them, 'til the tar was oozing in their eyes.

I heard those tar pits simmering on Sepulveda tonight;
around the corner from our house, a bullhorn amplified
the order to:

> *'GET OUT OF THE CAR!'*
> *'GET OUT OF THE CAR!'*

Our old dog Blue bayed out his warning,

from behind our granite walls,

where he stood bravely guarding

the plastic dinosaur in our pool.

When real dinosaurs were here

they could safely pause. Their

Tar Pits were announced

by rotting carcasses.

SUNDAY ON THE P.C.H.

Naked of its rider, the Harley still stood guard

the red smear beneath its wheels

slowly baking black in Sunday's heat.

Uniforms drew diagrams and waved thru gawkers

> on the Malibu P.C.H.

Lack of information troweled irritation

on two miles of backed-up drivers ignoring

the red-whined rescue sirening past them

> on the Malibu P.C.H.

When I returned, the uniforms were gone.

Drivers streamed by, unimpeded; blood,

tired through by traffic, no longer witnessed

> on the Malibu P.C.H.

SENSING MORNING ON A NOTED DAY

I awoke today, all my senses sensing
morning coffee, the light, the sheets
and birds, all of them good-morning-ing
the dawn in their own way.

Three years ago today, people leapt or fell
through their last morning to the streets
of New York. Was their last sensation
fear? Or was there some other
"we'll never know" last sensation?

I have lived three years more of sensing
my morning sensations. I have not had to leap.
I did not have to fall. Why not me?
Why them? Why anyone?

In 1941 the skies over Hawaii rained death
on the harbor named Pearl. For those not then
alive, it is now but a day the media notes.
When these, too are no more -- will it be noted, yet?

And what of 9/11 sixty years beyond?
Will it be noted still? Or are there terrors
yet unborn, which will serve to diminish its scale?

TIDES

The Timelessness of the Sea
is a verse God wrote to eternity
        believing that humanity could win.

Its certainty
bewilders me

on days when I am stunned
by incidents which prove
        it's in-humanity that's won.

A Fine Madness

We've a measure of fine madness,
allowing us to whisper of
the mystery by which we
still believe that we can be
                    humane.

If this madness could increase,
the tide of it would drown
the sanity by which we still
keep killing one another,
                    logically.

Bookplate Secrets Revealed
at the Newberry Library

The Bookplate, like Haiku, has boundaries which impose
upon the artist's moist intention, a structure that
condenses and reveals revelations that expanded
space or syllable would clumsily obscure. Bookplates play
where the night decays and camels walk on the moon,
investigating pageants pale pilgrims overlooked, while
planting dry-dated winter lies in purpled afternoons.

Inside the bookplate's confines, Adam's atoms are retrieved
and rearranged infinitely, in finite new erections resurrecting
men made pregnant with death windows which are worn
as if they're only a morning's monogram, parading molten
monarchs in Epistle's epitaphs, unfurling burdened banners
that ribbon into cherubs, crests and children, molting
yesterday's images to surprise someone today.

Unicorns of celadon reluctantly acknowledge they stroll upon a
dreamy esplanade, arranging erotic erasure on an ocean, mad and
silent, in the mindscape's breviary; where mountain ranges tour
around a leather-faced amoeba and blue wax feathered gargoyles
dwell on graven planets orbiting an anxious author's pen; where
fulsome fearful whispers weep their ungraped nightshade wine.

The bookplates' sun has rhythms rhyming wire flowers
roaming geometry's arcade, where maidens fold stray
vegetables of wizened marmalade and the Cherry Orchard's
portrait begs balloons at Shakespeare's Place, then stops to play at
horseshoes with envelopes of love, which flow in secret
inner tubes where rockets spray fresh laughing gas
on broken temple walls.

Chiseled stone and chariots once raced on the Acropolis
where they were set by artists to run for all eternity
on double-faced friezes that only God was 'sposed to see,
'til Elgin wrenched them out all naked, to quiver silently
and shudder on a bookplate where none would ever know
the psalms they meant to sing became just broken
hearts in stalactites made of rice.

The bookplate is the signal of the simple and the stern,
the plumber and philosopher and wistful waiting fauns.
Its lineage smells of cuneiform, of scrolls and temple bells,
pealing metal centuries, bathed in printer's ink,
inhaling etcher's acid, carving wooden blocks for books
that foiled the tyrant's torch, by the hand of hooded monks
who died a hundred times a life.

There are bookplates poised in an unborn synapse slice,
awaiting oxide vision and the breath of laser pulse,
directing it to intercept the universe's noon; that sits
there on its witless chip, drowning out the sound
of wooden players practicing an embryo in the shade
of Styx-shaped tentacles that fry in violet snow.

In the Beginning

"In the beginning,"
          said the ancient text,
"In the beginning, was Word."
But there had to have been,
before any word, a Thought
that was mother to word.

Word fleshed the thought
into atoms, shaping physics
which mothered existence;
where wholeness, set free,
divided itself, exploring
the wonder of novelty.

Then emerged light in which
          Thought
began to form its awesome
          Why.
"Why is Anything there
          at all?"

Did Anything ever answer?

At Peace In Santa Clarita

Nestled in the comfort of an ordinary
day was this afternoon, spent in your arms
which went on smiling into this night,
an ordinary night, as unaware of our
afternoon as of the crickets singing
in the hedge or of the lively
grandchildren playing at our feet.

For, on this day your body and your caring
released me to a beyond I did not know
was there and indelibly, on this afternoon,
your singularity became imprinted in my life.

Dare we hope these children at our feet,
in their maturity, will be as lucky as you
and me and to know for themselves,
as much as we know now.